LISTENING TO SILENCE

Michel Hubaut

Listening to silence

ST PAULS

Original title: *Les chemins du silence*
© 1991 Desclée de Brouwer, Paris, France

Translated by D. Mary Groves SDB

ST PAULS
Middlegreen, Slough SL3 6BT, United Kingdom
Moyglare Road, Maynooth, Co. Kildare, Ireland

English translation © ST PAULS (UK) 1994

ISBN 085439 478 8

Printed by Redwood, Trowbridge

ST PAULS is an activity of the priests and brothers of the Society of St Paul who proclaim the Gospel through the media of social communication

Contents

Noise has invaded our modern life like a sounding tidal wave, taking up every possible space. Drowned in the spume of words, tossed about at the whim of the media, thrown up like a shell on the surface of ourselves, we no longer know where we come from or where we are going. We have forgotten our own land. We have even forgotten the paths leading to our consciousness and the inner garden of the heart.

These few pages attempt to show how the silence which is much more than a simple absence of noise is not a luxury reserved to monks or a few ivory-tower thinkers but a necessity as vital for us all as the air we breathe and the bread we eat. Not only is it a matter of personal identity but also of the quality of relationships and the future life of the whole of society.

1

We have lost the key

Occasionally at a bend of the busy road, submerged in the roar of traffic, there still stands out an unfamiliar sign: 'Silence – Hospital'. Sometimes still between the speeches and the bugle call before a cenotaph we are invited to observe the minute's silence. Is silence today to be reserved to the sick and the dead? It must indeed be recognised that places and times of silence are more and more rare in the daily life of our contemporaries. And even in the country, with the mechanisation of farming operations the silence of the ploughman slowly following behind his peaceful shire horses had long been no more than a painting by, say, a Constable.

My intention is in no way to cultivate some conservative longing for the good old days but to take a clear-eyed look at a social and cultural revolution which as always can produce the best and the worst of futures for the human race.

News-flash as we jump out of bed. Marathon to get to work. Grinding of machines or buzzing of computers. Telephones ringing. Noisy canteen or restaurant. Again jostled by the crowds on the underground or commuter platforms to return home. Television non-stop.

A so-called place of leisure where the decibels of band or stereo reach hallucinatory intensity. And those transistors which pursue you even on the holiday beaches...

Thirsting for silence we run the risk of living not only

on the periphery of ourselves but also of reducing every human relationship to cold and superficial social convention. We see already on various levels how the absence of interiority has complex personal and social consequences.

Numerous symptoms, more or less serious, have been analysed by psychologists, sociologists and educationists. Torn from their own deep roots, couples, families, social groups necessarily find personal fragility and instability reacting on their lives. Children have difficulty in concentrating. Relationships become superficial. Increase in consumption of tranquillisers or sleeping pills. Chronic inability to adapt, low tolerance threshold. Depression. Breakdown. Mad search for an escape, drugs, sects...

The confusion, the emptiness experienced by so many of our contemporaries shows that the human race has probably lost out on an essential dimension. How to be oneself without plumbing one's heights and depths, without remaining quiet? Silence at different levels, physical, psychological, spiritual, makes for a balanced existence and growth. Anyone who has not integrated silence not only loses the art of living, a quality of life, but a structural element at the deepest part of human nature.

Kierkegaard used to say : 'If I were a doctor and my advice asked I should reply: Advocate silence, make people be quiet.' So do we have to start 'silence therapy' funded by social security like rest cures for modern people to rediscover the virtues of silence?

2

In praise of true rest

A bolt is shot back in our breast And a lost pulse of
feeling starts up again.
The eye sinks inward, and the heart lies plain.
And what we mean, we say, and what we would, we
know.
A man becomes aware of his life's flow...
And hears its winding murmur, and he sees
the meadows where it glides, the sun, the breeze.
And there arrives a lull in the hot race Within he doth
forever chase
That flying and elusive shadow: Rest...
And then he thinks he knows The Hills where his life
rose,
And the Sea where it goes.

Matthew Arnold

More and more of our contemporaries are reconsider-
ing this truth. They feel the urgent necessity for their
peace of mind to make a break from time to time in the
whirlwind rhythm of modern life. For the first level of
silence is quite simply a need in the physical and psychological order.

A young businessman confided to me: 'It was as
though I was jammed in spite of myself in the grind of
social and professional obligations, caught between pay-
ing the mortgage and the threat of redundancy. I had the
strange sensation of going through life on board a high

speed train which never stopped anywhere and I was going to rush into the buffers of death without time to admire the countryside. I sometimes joined my family for a few days on holiday, taking my files with me... It took a serious bout of ill-health to make me dare to pull the emergency cord on that phantom train, stop off in the open country and take time to go and pick wild flowers with my children.'

It is imperative for us to find the paths of silence again. The first level of this silence is at everyone's command. There is no need to read learned treatises about it. Don't wait to crack before finding another way to live at intervals at least. For example, make holidays a real time of rest for body and mind, the first stage of detoxification from noise.

Savour simple pleasures again. Walk very early in the morning along the beach. Breath through every pore the scents of your native air.

Listen to the dull roar of the waves or the regular lapping of ebb and flow of our millenary story. Listen to the silence of mountains under snow and their majesty telling of human littleness, and grandeur too, since we have the capacity to contemplate them.

Wander in the country. Prefer winding lanes to casino lights. Ramble to the source of a stream. Admire the delicate veining of a leaf, the busy skill of an ant, the perfection of a flower, a spider's web dew-decked with pearls of light.

Find enjoyment again in taking time off for a lazy free morning. Lie in the grass at the foot of a great tree. There, face up to the sky, be caressed by the wind, take in the gentle swaying of the branches. Think of nothing. Simply be a tree. Take on the vital energy of the sap rising from the roots and mounting on up to the leafy canopy. For a few moments become again the amazing conjunction of mineral, vegetable and animal worlds.

Enjoy a chat with an old man sitting in his doorway. Join in a game of bowls with the locals. Find again simple ways to be happy and find pleasure in the slow and the unexpected in daily life. Experience the charm of a dim little church where you had to get the key from a lady living nearby. Be quiet. Quiet. Plunge into silence as into a refreshing bath.

Be free of the tyranny of the TV to take up family ties again, so often stretched by the demands of work schedules. Relax and laugh together. Have a game of scrabble. Take the smallest by the hand and run into the wind across scented heath or read the latest comic aloud sitting on the ground with the child.

But we shall see that this physical relaxation is only a stage. Silence is not only an absence of noise. It has to be accompanied by a psychological silence so as to open up other levels of silence, those of the consciousness and the soul or the heart listening to the Spirit.

3

The music of silence

Thinkers of antiquity explained the 'radiant face of a new-born child' by the fact that the soul could still hear the echo of the music of the spheres, the heavenly music from inter-stellar space it had just passed through. The Fathers of the Church wrote that the human being, micro-cosm of the created universe, could hear in the silence of the soul the harmonious music of the whole of creation. And the traditional symbolic portrayal of multitudes of angel-musicians twixt heaven and earth playing on their instruments an imperceptible and eternal music also sig-nifies that the cosmic universe is an immense symphony in which every creature, animate or inanimate, executes its score for the greater glory of the Creator.

In fact, absolute silence destroys us. To be within our human capacity it has to be a tissue of unobtrusive sounds, their alternation or combination producing a peaceful harmonious chorus. The first stage of an ap-prenticeship to silence often consists in relearning how to detect these thousand and one little notes which make up the music of silence.

Silence is a school for training or rather retraining our attention to the music of creation. Human beings are no longer spontaneously attentive to things and other be-ings and they have to learn to live and let live without first seeking to explain or utilise. Watch and listen to a tree, a flower, a pebble. Let the object express itself in the silence. Let it 'speak'. Receive, do not take.

While not necessarily being a thinker or a poet, who

has never heard the music of silence? The silence of mountains under snow. Silence of the setting sun. And even silence of a rolling sea.

We have to begin by taking the time to stop and stand. Time to cleanse the ears as though detoxifying an addiction. Listen to the soughing of the wind, the crackle of the fire, the song of a grasshopper or a bird, a murmuring stream, familiar village sounds or those at home, sounds which do not break the silence but weave it. Only an aggressive noise spoils it.

Listen to a piece of music as though you were a simple child hearing it for the first time. Not judging, not analysing. Let yourself be penetrated by the sonorities, the colours of sound.

Anyone who no longer knows how to listen to the music of creation will not know how to listen to others and still less to the silence of God.

Silence is like a musical rest which allows us to hear what goes before and after. It prepares the quality of our presence to another and the depth of our encounter. Silence is a school of respect. Respect for creation. Respect for others…

Silence teaches us to listen: to listen to the music of creation so as to catch its hidden harmony. Listen to our heart, our consciousness for a better understanding of ourselves and be able to direct our lives. Listen to other people so as to be enriched by their diversity and love them better. Listen to God, his inner Word, his Spirit, who speaks in our heart to give us life.

Listen, but also feel, touch, regain contact with basic matter. Turn over the soil. Handle a pebble. Walk barefoot on the sand. Scuffle through leaves or pine needles under the trees. Everything can become a school for learning attentiveness, presence to creation, to others and to ourselves. This is the first stage, which leads on to other levels of silence.

15

Like a beating heart

Thus even before reflecting on the spiritual dimension we can say that silence is a physical and psychological element of the human person. For our growth to be harmonious it must necessarily be structured in two complementary directions: without and within. We do not become ourselves except through holding in balance this twofold movement: exteriorisation, relationship to others, to the world; and interiorisation, withdrawal, silence, reflection. A little like the alternating movements of the heart as it contracts and expands with a regular beat.

That is why I consider silence to be one of the fundamental human rights to be defended as much as peace. So we must fight against anything which prevents a person from integrating this essential element of the self. Put this before those responsible for town planning, land management, transport networks. Arrange for places of peace and quiet in the community. Open the churches, which are not primarily museum pieces but places for silence and adoration. In religion classes teach the children to develop their natural capacity for interiority. Monasteries should be more and more open as schools where silence is lived. Priests need to become increasingly familiar with meditation and masters of spirituality.

If social interaction in our societies is not accompanied by an increase of interiorisation we face serious imbalances. It is a question of human happiness, integral development of the individual and of the quality of relationships. And so initiation into silence and the interior life is a missionary priority for the Church today. Help communities to create friendly spaces for silence and prayer, as lungs preventing our towns and cities from suffocation.

It has been repeatedly said, and rightly, that Christianity is no longer conceivable without a resolute attack being made on hunger, injustice and violence which degrade the human race and offend against God's loving design. In our day it has been said equally strongly that Christianity is not to be conceived without having an equally determined commitment to restore to humanity its inner dimension.

The human enigma:
a being of solitude and relationships

That said, we have to acknowledge that the main obstacle to silence, however indispensable it may be to our physical, psychological and spiritual health, is not the environment but ourselves. We seem to flee this silence which is yet so vital. Not the least of human paradoxes? To throw light on this puzzle we can have recourse to the insights of the human sciences and of the Judeo-Christian revelation.

Any psychologist will tell you that men and women are by nature social beings who need to live with others, by means of others, and for others. And in this sense, they can experience solitude as a psychologically hostile state, against nature, which they instinctively seek to avoid by every means.

First point: Solitude must not be confused with isolation. A child isolated on a desert island, even with everything necessary for bodily development, will have little chance of realising its identity and being present to itself. Further, we well know the psychological harm done by certain forms of solitude suffered by the old or by prisoners, for example.

The solitude which is isolation is also sometimes the result of closing in on oneself, out of fear of encountering others, of forming relationships. Every kind of isolation quickly becomes unbearable and can sometimes even lead to suicide. The wisdom of the Bible makes

God say at creation: it is not good that the man should be alone' (Gen 2:18). But we shall see that if isolation destroys, true solitude is constructive.

So men and women spontaneously aim to communicate, to relate. Their whole being is structured toward meeting one another. Some psychoanalysts see in this essentially relational structure of the human being one of the bases of our childish terrors at being alone. They act as an instinctive alarm signal that there is indeed danger.

But, and this is where the paradox arises, the desire to be present to the other is rarely fulfilled. Apart from infrequent times of 'communion', we very quickly make the sad discovery that there will always be between us and the other, even the most intimate other, something which is incommunicable, an unbridgeable distance.

Each one is a unique being with a secret garden which will always remain in part impenetrable, inexpressible. Any dream of fusion is doomed since it fails to recognise the other's difference and thus identity is denied.

Writers like Jean-Paul Sartre, pushing this statement to extremes, have described *ad nauseam* this non-communication between people: 'Until the end we shall remain alone together' (*Huis clos*). And they go so far as to say that 'hell is other people'.

So a person can bear neither complete isolation nor the continual presence of others. A prolonged solitude arouses an inconsolable desire for the presence of others. Permanent community living, an intensely relational life, creates a desire for solitude. This alternation of presence and solitude appears to be a fundamental principle of personal equilibrium. Solitude and presence even call for each other. The quality and depth of the one conditions the other.

19

6

Strange and radical incompleteness

Presence and solitude are a pair, indissoluble from the mystery which is the human being. But neither the one nor the other suffices of itself.

This apparent duality manifests the ontological structure of the human personality which as we have seen needs this binary rhythm of going out of self and return to self. But here is also a sign of the existential human drama. A person is that strange ever restless being finding no peace either in solitude, seized by anguish, or in the presence of others, which does not satisfy and is so illusory. We find neither in ourselves nor in others the fullness we seek.

This is not accidental but the manifestation of a radical incompleteness hungering for the Absolute. It is an ontological incompleteness impelling us to that perpetual search, now in solitude now in relationships, after rest and a happiness which always escapes us. Complete solitude supposes a completeness, a self-sufficiency, which we do not have. And relationship cannot fulfil our desire since others are not absolute either. Aristotle had already realised that solitude cannot be a state of blessedness save for the divinity whose plenitude suffices to itself.

It is here that the Judeo-Christian revelation throws definite light on the human enigma.

Indeed, the personhood of Christ, who claims to be Son of the Father indwelt by the Spirit, reveals to us that God is not a solitary being but relational, a communion of love between persons. The Christian belief is in God one and three. This unveiling of God's inmost mystery, while remaining inexpressible, appears none the less a necessary consequence of the mystery of love which demands love in return, an interpersonal relationship.

The other corollary in revelation concerns the human being. In fact, inasmuch as we are created in the image of the triune God we are by nature relational beings. It is not possible for us to exist, develop, be persons except in and through the exercise of relationship: loving and being loved. To be relational is a constituent of our being, our identity. Our whole being is as though straining toward that final end which is the fullness of divine love.

It is surely in relying on the revelation as confirmed by Christ's incarnation that many Christians consider God is not to be found by a 'flight into the desert' but by a sharing in the human condition as it is found in the pattern of daily relationships. Human love, then, opening out and giving itself to others is where in their eyes God most often speaks and reveals himself.

But though we are not all called to be hermits we do need to discern the significance of the attraction to solitude found in the great monastic traditions since the beginning of Christianity, in the West as in the East. The fruits of it in the lives of saints are too evident to be denied. The great spiritual writers have always unanimously recognised solitude as playing an important role in human formation. *O beata solitudo!*

But we shall see, as we partly have already, that it is not a question of opposition but of complementarity. Human beings are both solitary and gregarious and therefore need solitude and relationships in order to find themselves and to find God.

Such a writer as Saint-Exupéry understood this well since he praises friendship and exalts solitude. And

Charles de Foucauld lost in the far desert is universally considered a brother to all.

No doubt we shall also find that solitude, like relationships, has its illusions and snares. But the ambiguity always springs from our human nature. We shall see how in the end the sole criterion for discernment will always be the quality of love as practised. Relationships like solitude are at our service when we learn to love. 'Where are love and loving-kindness, God is there.'

Both the two paths, solitude and relationship, must remain by nature limited except when open to God in his fullness. Silence for a believer is not primarily a space but a quality of the heart, and solitude is never isolation or evasion or flight but a new attentiveness to a Presence dwelling equally in the solitude of the desert and in human relationships.

Inhabited silence builds up; isolation destroys

olitude and liberty when inextricably linked are like fire, which can heat or destroy, purify or burn, bring life or death. Solitude can be a an opportunity or a danger, a spur or a poison...

Purveyors of tourism have spread the idea that solitude could be harmful. Solitude is in fact not a purely negative reality. It can be the best and the worst of things: 'Invaluable friend, mortal enemy, solitude restores, solitude destroys... It drives us to our limits and beyond' (Françoise Dolto). If solitude and silence are often closely linked in the Christian tradition, voluntary solitude, temporary or permanent, which can be constructive and enriching, is never to be confused with the silence of isolation, which always impoverishes and destroys.

This is the reason why within Christianity solitude and silence are not values or an end in themselves. Silence is a path to the heart indwellt by the Spirit, the absolute Love of God. And in the plenitude of this ineffable Presence we are truly present to our self, to the world and to others.

Silent solitude must serve to encounter the One who is there to meet us, not in sterile narcissistic introspection but in a loving dialogue which puts us in communion with all people and the whole earth. Our age often talks about freedom, liberation, and does not seem to realise that it is this very open solitude which has forged the greatest men and women of action, the most creative thinkers and the most ardent saints.

Only an 'inhabited silence' is compatible with the make-up and creation of the human race. If the presence of God there ceases to be recognised or sought, solitude becomes inhuman. It is almost impossible to love silence and live serenely in solitude without a belief in the inner dimension of humanity and of the world, without being open to transcendence.

If silence looks to solitude and solitude invites silence, a happy conjunction of the two is not automatic. It is possible to make a great deal of noise in your heart in the middle of the desert and be silent in the midst of a crowd. You can be filled with yourself and your problems in a monastery, and fully available in the heart of society. More than a space into which to retreat, silence is an interior attitude.

Experience shows that there are fruitful silences outside solitude, and solitudes with no true silence. We often meet men and women who blame the noisy, busy world for their 'dis-ease' and long for solitude. But as soon as they are, perhaps in spite of themselves, thrown into a solitude imposed by unforeseen circumstances, they complain even more. No sooner have they the solitude they so longed for as a place to be free than it becomes more intolerable than the bustle and noise.

Tumultuous desires and obsessive frustrations have followed them. They feel weighed down, at the mercy of contradictory whims. They have not found true silence in such a solitude but a huge boredom, a deadly void which threatens in the end to unhinge them. So we sometimes long for solitude because we think we shall have a relief from noise. True enough on the psychological plane at first, by contrast, but rarely for long if all we find there is ourselves. In this case it very soon becomes solitude not noise which is 'hell'.

Desert-lovers

However, without necessarily going back to the anchorites of the first centuries, contemporaries such as Psichari and Saint-Exupéry have shown how silence, particularly in the desert, was for them a special place for human and spiritual maturity, a school of truth and love.

'I used to say to myself: it will be time to withdraw into myself when I am back in the cold of Europe. For now, we'll let silence take over. It is a great teacher of truth. To these great silent spaces lying athwart my life I owe all I may ever have of good in me. Woe to those who have never known silence! The silence which can do harm and can do good, good and bad together. Silence like a smoothly gliding stream, like a beautiful full-flowing river...

'Very often silence has come to me like a beloved teacher, and it seemed a little of heaven descending on humankind to make them better. In vast sheets it would come down from heaven, great inter-stellar spaces, unwavering panoply of the cold moon. It came from the back of space, from beyond time, from before the worlds were and will no longer be...

'Then I would stop full of love and respect. For silence also teaches love... The absence of sounds is so restful. But silence is more than that. It is a great African plain swept by the biting wind, it is the Indian Ocean, night under the stars. This was the silence Paschal heard by night at Port Royal, and as I have sometimes met it in the African wastes. At such times we know that it alone, alas, came from God.

'It was then I knew my first real times of solitude; it was then that for the first time in the eternal silence of the desert I marked the slow passing of the hours. In that dead land where no one has ever lived for long, I seemed to go beyond the ordinary bounds of life, and to advance, trembling with vertigo, to the edge of eternity' (E. Psichari).

Saint-Exupéry experienced something similar: 'I will write a hymn to silence... God watching over our feverishness, God's mantle over human fret... It is good to find in God the silence of eternity.

'Haven of silence. Silence in God where all our ships find haven... Strange that love should begin only there where expectation is at an end. Love is first of all an activity of prayer and prayer activates silence... When one day, Lord, you harvest your creation, open up to us your double doors and have us enter where there will be nothing to reply because there will be no further response save beatitude which is the key-stone to all our questioning and the sight which satisfies.'

He found that in silence love asks no more questions but opens to the mystery of God and God replies by freeing the soul from the questioning which prevents it from hearing. He discovered too with his new companions of the desert that silence is indeed the spiritual space which channels deep human relationships, with no more need for words, so often a source of misunderstanding. 'They and I, we were now only a prayer melting into the silence of God.'

These two writers, differing in their spiritual journey, give proof of a desert experience which matured them and made them outstanding testimonies to silence and solitude.

26

Not everyone is called to withdraw into the desert or to a monastic cloister. But we all have a vital need of silence. We must therefore conclude that God grants to each one the necessary form of solitude or desert. How many believers, men and women, have without necessarily being Carthusians experienced this new dimension. 'The silence of the room where I am writing is one of the greatest riches of my life' (Julien Green).

We shall see how anyone wanting to 'keep silence' in order to listen to God and make life whole must learn to go down even in the city into the 'inner desert' of the heart where the Spirit is waiting.

Did not Christ say that every follower of his is in the world without being entirely of the world (Jn 17). Faith, which reveals a person's depths and widens horizons, necessarily creates a kind of distancing in the order of daily life. Touched by a Word of fire which sets the heart on fire we can no longer make an absolute of finite human things. Nothing is despised, but everything becomes relative.

This break with solid reality, detachment within attachment, so remarkable in the lives of all the saints, is the fruit of faith and love.

Profoundly present to their contemporaries they are nevertheless by grace citizens of 'another world', invisible but more real than any human reality.

Experience shows that the grace of God alone can make of solitude a 'living-space' for interior silence, which unlocks a person's innermost life where the Spirit breathes and God speaks.

The school of the desert

What we have just said is but a translation into modern terms of the Judeo-Christian tradition where the 'desert experience' with its strong implication of silence and solitude has a central place. A decisive experience to be handed down. The Exodus which marked the birth of the People of the Covenant.

Already in the Bible the desert evokes contradictory images. A land accursed where life is rarely found and human beings survive with difficulty, it is in symbol the place of evil beasts, hostile forces, demons, death. But paradoxically the desert is also in the collective consciousness of the people of the Bible, the time and place to come to a new freedom where the limits of the possible are pushed back, and to be aware of a transcendent and intimate God who is burning fire and a gentle breeze entering into their history.

Those forty years of wandering in the desert symbolise life's span. The space of time necessary for a person to discover through manifold hunger and thirst the one true bread and the one true spring of living water able to impart eternal life.

The biblical writers saw in the Hebrew people a word-event of revelation. This 'wandering in the desert' is the God of the Covenant teaching by an enduring example. It concerns us still. For who among us (what people, what Church) does not know at one time or another in our history a terrible solitude, a 'desert experience' which forces us to ask the basic questions about our personal and collective destiny?

Every 'desert experience' is at once a testing and a privileged time. A test which strips us of our masks, our lies, our false security. A privileged time when we are made simple, stripped, no longer able to cheat, and we are brought to admit the truth of our radical poverty and our finiteness, to sense the nearness of God, to realise our true hunger, our true thirst.

It is the time to realise that the human being is incomplete and in search of a fulfilment beyond individual possibilities alone, a being with a hunger for the Absolute.

The journey of the Hebrew people from slavery to freedom, and that of Christ at Easter from death to resurrection, cast light on our 'deserts' and our inexhaustible hunger for the Promised Land, the Father's Kingdom.

So to take a few 'desert days' alone or in a monastery is to live from time to time through a symbolic gathering up of the whole of our life's journey during which we have sometimes had to undergo dramatic desert experiences. It is rarely given to us to choose our own 'desert'. It is a different one for each of us. But sooner or later we have to cross it.

At the personal level it might be a time of moral testing or a breakdown in health , a time of doubt, aridity, separation, stress. At the level of the Church it can be the experience of being reduced to a Church of Silence, martyred or sleeping... On the collective level this desert experience can be that of an oppressed minority, a people torn apart by war or endemic underdevelopment.

There is a desert for the married couple. There is the desert of the cloister. A desert for the believer. Desert of silence. Desert of loneliness. Desert of heart or mind. No two desert experiences are alike but there are always many features in common with the model supplied by the journey of the people of the Covenant.

This 'solitude' time is part of the paschal journey of every life. A time when each of us, even the prodigal child, remembers that life is an exodus towards the Promised Land, the country of perfect love, one vast return to the Father's house.

It is a solitude which reminds us that to be converted is to move out of oneself each morning, step aside from the limelight, take a new direction, so as to go out to our Father and our brothers and sisters. A solitude during which we are all, every nation, every community, every one of us, called to relive the fundamental choices offered to the Hebrew people and to Christ in the desert.

It takes a whole life-time for a person to discover that in the midst of all our desires the real hunger is to be loved and to love for eternity, and that the only true bread which can satisfy our hunger is God the Absolute, his word, his life, his love.

Finally left to ourselves, we find our hungers to be fairly elementary. For centuries the hopes of the People of God have hardly gone beyond looking for a good fat land and abundant flocks.

Only a few prophetic figures, inspired by the Spirit, will be there to drive them to analyse their real hunger.

Like the Hebrews complaining in the desert we would often prefer the taste of the bread of servitude. Slave bread comes in many forms. Bread of ease. Bread of comfort. Bread of routine. Coward's bread. Bread of compromise... So to examine what is our real hunger we need that time in the 'desert', chosen or accepted.

We need a hard and blessed solitude which shows us that human greatness is to go on, from one camping ground to the next, never done with passing on from slavery to the land of freedom.

The solitude of our 'deserts' is always that time when confronted with harsh reality we each complain like the Hebrews, voice the great human complaint: Is there a God out there and if so does he really go with us? (cf Ex 17:7).

10

The bright face
and the dark face of silence

From earliest antiquity thinkers and moralists have often recalled the many benefits of silence for individual and collective life. Already Plutarch wrote: 'I have never repented of having kept silent but often of speaking too much.' And even popular wisdom accepts that 'speech is silver, silence is gold.'

And so in all cultures there are maxims to garner about silence being discretion which does not shout another's weaknesses from the rooftops, refrains from tarnishing a neighbour's reputation. The silence of the patience which knows precisely that there is a time to speak and a time to keep silent. The silence of prudence which weighs words and does not judge too hastily. The silence of compassion which more by actions than by words witnesses to a sincere affection towards one hurt in body or heart. The silence of humility which accepts that human reason and intelligence have their limits and recognises a higher light.

In the Christian tradition the Fathers of the Desert and the great spiritual writers gave over whole chapters in honour of silence, often considered as the seed-ground of the theological virtues – faith, hope and charity – life in the Spirit and holiness. Drawing on their own experience they made of silence an incomparable teacher of attention to God and to others, thus predisposing to adoration and service.

But if we should greatly esteem silence as a friend to humanity, we have also to beware of its caricatures. For silence in a person is ambivalent, as is everything human. Not all silence is automatically virtuous or healthy, nor a sign of wisdom or an interior life. Silent people are to be found among saints and among criminals.

Enough here to recall a few examples from the gallery of caricatures of silence and forms of silence which are bad. Indifference, for which others are merely adjuncts to an egoistical life. The scornful silence, which looks down on one from the heights of its superiority. The stoic silence, which 'masters' itself as illustrated by the famous lines of Alfred de Vigny: 'Silence alone is great and all the rest weakness… Groan, weep, pray, all are equally cowardly.'

The haughty silence of self-sufficient grandeur which responds, as Vigny also says, 'by a cold silence to the silence of the divinity'. The silence of pride which refuses to honour and admire the good others say or do. The silence of laziness which will make no effort towards a relationship. The silence of the fool who has nothing to say but would like it to be considered proof of deep thought, whereas 'the silence of fools is a locked cupboard without a key.'

The silence of bitterness, mulling over its wrongs and not wanting to renew contact. The silence of weakness in fear of becoming involved. The silence of cowardice which takes care not to be compromised. The silence of complicity which acquiesces in secret. The traitorous silence which fails to give expected support.

So, just as with people, there are good and bad silences which reflect two faces, dark and light. By silence we can be purified, unified, but also destroyed.

Our silence, then, can show respect or scorn, love or hate, joy or suffering, reflection or stupidity, autism or sensitiveness... How are we to distinguish for example between the refusal to speak of the taciturn, the sullen, the bitter, the misanthropist, the one turned in on self, and the silence of the wise? The first way of telling what is our kind of silence is to discern the quality of our love, our relations with God and with others.

11

Silence in the Bible

There is a time to keep silence and a time to speak' (Eccl 3:7).

In the old Testament writings as a whole, silence is not much in evidence. Here and there we find references, the attentive silence of Abraham's servant (Gen 24:21), the grieving silence of Jacob on hearing of his daughter's rape (Gen 34:35), or the prostrate silence of a man overcome by misfortune: 'The elders of daughter Zion sit on the ground in silence; they have thrown dust on their heads and put on sackcloth' (Lam 2:10).

In contrast, wisdom literature makes frequent references. The Old Testament sages like to develop this theme of silence which sometimes appears as the obverse of a calculated prudence or simply a part of social behaviour. 'Be brief; say much in few words; be as one who knows and can still hold his tongue. Among the great do not act as their equal, and when another is speaking do not babble' (Sir 32:8-9).

But above all it seems that the wise man in the Bible has an instinctive mistrust of speech. 'When words are many, transgression is not lacking, but the prudent are restrained in speech' (Prov 10:19); 'with their mouth the godless would destroy their neighbours, a group goes about telling secrets, but an intelligent person remains silent' (Prov 11:9; 12:13); 'the righteous hate falsehood' (Prov 13:5) but the wicked defame and dishonour; 'the more words the more vanity' (Eccl 6:11).

One who speaks too much will with difficulty avoid shallowness, backbiting, detraction and calumny. 'Those who guard their mouths preserve their lives, those who open wide their lips come to ruin' (Prov 13:3). Or again, one who cannot refrain from speech is like an open city without walls.

Beware of the inopportune word. 'There is a rebuke that is untimely, and there is the person who is wise enough to keep silent. Some people keep silent and are thought to be wise while others are detested for being talkative. Some people keep silent because they have nothing to say, while others keep silent because they know when to speak. The wise remain silent until the right moment but a boastful fool misses the right moment (cf Sir 20:1,5-7).

A flood of bad words not only sullies the reputation of others but pollutes our own heart. The ravages of calumny, of the untamed tongue, are well illustrated by this little Breton anecdote:

A woman had accused herself in confession of gossiping about her neighbours. The village curé gave her as penance to pluck a goose on top of a hill in a high wind. This she did. But when she came to give an account of it, her curé then told her to go back and pick up all the feathers.

– But, monsieur le curé, that is impossible now. They are all blown away in all directions and some of them well past the village!

– My child, replied the wise curé, so it is with words of calumny or detraction. You will never bring them back.

Silence can also be the sign of a generous heart indulgent towards the weaknesses of others: 'Whoever belittles another lacks sense, but an intelligent person remains silent' (Prov 11:12). It is goodness, love, respect for others, which will keep us from hawking around and spreading some scandal or unhappy recollection, so as not to overwhelm one already wounded. Courtesy and tact are often companions of silence.

And before the sorrow or suffering of a brother, a sister, a friend, silence is better, as Job told his visitors who loaded him with words of consolation: 'If you would only keep silent, that would be your wisdom!' (Job 13:5).

It is difficult not to answer insult with insult or respond to an invective with an outburst. It takes great strength of soul to know how to keep quiet in an argument when feelings run away with reason. Wounded pride naturally seeks to get the mastery. It is not easy to keep quiet when sure one is in the right.

Especially is it difficult to keep quiet when the unscrupulous or evil person seems to triumph: 'I said: I will guard my ways that I may not sin with my tongue; I will keep a muzzle on my mouth as long as the wicked are in my presence. I was silent and still, I held my peace to no avail; my distress grew worse, my heart became hot within me. While I mused the fire burned; then I spoke with my tongue' (Ps 39:2-4).

No doubt it is not good to let people walk all over one. Self-defence is sometimes a matter of dignity and justice. But the strength of a silent person lies in not letting oneself be carried away by uncontrollable anger and knowing when it is time to reply.

Do we not often regret speaking on impulse without taking time to weigh our words?

Sometimes silence will speak louder than words. We may judge that to speak will not for the time being further truth or love, because our brother or sister is not in the right frame of mind to listen.

Finally, for the wise man in the Bible, this purely

human wisdom is itself a gift from God who helps us to discern the time for silence and the time to speak. 'Set a guard over my mouth, O Lord; keep watch over the door of my lips' (Ps 141:3).

Master your tongue as a sea-captain directs his ship by the rudder

There is also the silence of faith before the surpassing mystery of the world or the action of God. 'Therefore the prudent will keep silence in such a time; for it is an evil time' (Am 5:13). Such as the silence of Job who realised after discoursing at length in vain: 'See, I am of small account; what shall I answer you? I lay my hand on my mouth...' (Job 40:4), or of the just man hoping for the ultimate triumph, beyond the ruin of his people and their trials, of the Creator and Master of the human story: 'The Lord is good to those who wait for him, to the soul that seeks him. It is good that one should wait quietly for the salvation of the Lord... to sit alone in silence when the Lord has imposed it' (Lam 3:25ff).

The silence of the faithful in the Bible is neither resigned submission nor despair but in spite of trials patient confidence in the Lord's love and fidelity.

Analysis such as this of the benefits of silence is scarcely to be found in the New Testament. But we may point out this long passage from the Letter of St James which uniquely echoes the wisdom type of thinking.

'If any think they are religious and do not bridle their tongues, their religion is worthless...

'Anyone who makes no mistakes in speaking is perfect, able to keep the whole body in check with a bridle. If we put bits into the mouths of horses to make them obey us, we guide their whole bodies. Or look at ships: though they are so large that it takes strong winds to drive them, yet they are guided by a very small rudder wherever the will of the pilot directs. So also the tongue is a small member, yet it boasts of great exploits. How great a forest is set ablaze by a small fire! And the tongue is a fire...

'For every species of beast and bird, of reptile and sea creature can be tamed and has been tamed by the human species, but no one can tame the tongue — a restless evil, full of deadly poison.

'With it we bless the Lord and Father, and with it we curse those who are made in the likeness of God. From the same mouth come blessing and cursing. My brothers and sisters, this ought not to be so. Does a spring pour forth from the same opening both fresh and brackish water? Can a fig tree, my brothers and sisters, yield olives, or a grapevine figs? No more can salt water yield fresh' (Jas 1:26 and 3:1-12).

Language is one of the excellences of the human race, masterpiece of creation. Our words, whether for good or ill, always carry the fragrance or bad odour of the inner source from which they spring: the human heart.

And there is a time to speak

'There is a time to keep silence and a time for speaking' (Eccl 3:7).

If a wise person accepts that truth rarely proceeds out of a fit of anger, there is no hesitation in breaking silence to give a frank explanation. This is preferable to any kind of suppressed brooding which destroys inner peace. 'How much better it is to rebuke than to fume' (Sir 20:2).

It is sometimes better to bring things to a head than to keep up a misunderstanding or let some rumour go round: 'Question a friend; perhaps he did not do it... Question a neighbour; perhaps he did not say it... Question a friend for perhaps it is slander, so do not believe everything you hear. A person may make a slip without intending it, and who has not sinned with his tongue?' (Sir 19:13-17).

The biblical prophets, moreover, are not tender towards those leaders and pastors of the children of God who shirk responsibility by a guilty silence: 'Israel's sentinels are blind, are all without knowledge; they are all silent dogs that cannot bark; dreamily lying down, loving to slumber' (Is 56:10).

And no doubt it is not for nothing that in the New Testament one of the names for the Devil is 'dumb spirit', from whom Jesus freed a man so that he could regain the use of speech (Mt 9:32,33).

The Devil can use silence for his own ends. So there is a 'devilish silence'. The Father of Lies is capable of making us dumb, shut in on ourselves, our life closed to the truth, to witness, to praise.

But as St Paul writes, no one can fetter the Word of God. For centuries, in spite of persecutions and trials, many Christians have heard the urgent call which God addresses to the apostle of the nations: "Do not be afraid, but speak and do not be silent, for I am with you…' (Acts 18:9-10).

And in the face of his detractors who would like to reduce him to silence St Paul, charged with proclaiming the Gospel, always refuses to tone down God's word and collude with what he calls shameful silences.

'Therefore, since it is by God's mercy that we are engaged in this ministry, we do not lose heart. We have renounced the shameful things that are hidden, we refuse to practise cunning or to falsify God's word… But just as we have the same spirit that is in accordance with Scripture – I believed and so I spoke – we also believe, and so we speak, because we know that the one who has raised the Lord Jesus will raise us also with Jesus' (2 Cor 4:1-2 and 13-14).

And in the name of the mystery of Christ's incarnation and his kingdom, he does not hesitate to write to one of his disciples: 'Proclaim the message; be persistent whether the time is favourable or unfavourable; convince, rebuke, and encourage, with the utmost patience in teaching' (2 Tim 4:1-4).

But we need to have practised inner silence, let ourselves be moulded by the word of Christ, for a long time before daring to reprove a brother or sister who has turned aside from the Way, dare to make a fraternal exhortation, just, well-founded, animated by a real love of the other. 'Love and truth embrace', says the psalmist. Anyone aiming to 'speak the truth' without loving, risks becoming insupportable, dogmatic; and one who seeks to love without care for the truth risks complicity in cowardly silences.

We need to have long welcomed the Spirit of Love in the silence of the heart in order to be able to speak a true word to a brother or sister, a word capable of inviting conversion and bringing about progress in the other person without humiliation or discouragement. Moreover one of the signs that our fraternal exhortation does come from the Spirit is that it does not disturb our own inner silence.

The silence of conscience and heart

It is first of all on the level of an interior dialogue with ourselves that we attempt to read and understand our own story, our past, our present, our plans, and attempt to analyse our successes and failures, our dreams and illusions, our joys and sorrows. We must in short integrate our life as it progresses, or become a cork bobbing on the passing waves of time.

In the silence of conscience there starts up an interior debate between several voices, the result being our choices, our decisions. This is the sanctum of our free-will. The debate is between the better and the less good in ourselves, about the values we hold or reject. It is the place where we try to decipher our own mystery, our true identity and our destiny.

In a person who has left this silence zone, conscience becomes lifeless and no longer reacts except superficially, on the emotional level, skin-deep. It becomes the plaything of slogans, fashions, opinion. Without that inner debate in the silence of conscience there is no true personality.

It would be entirely artificial to seek to establish divisions between silence of the senses, psychological silence, silence of conscience and the silence of the heart. Interactions between all these levels are complex. That said, our dialogue with our own consciences, however stirring and necessary, is not to be confused with the silence of the heart.

We have a tendency, especially in the West, to oppose heart and head. The head is said to be the area of the cerebral, the mental, the intellectual, logical and rational. And the heart is the seat of the emotions. Now the heart in the Judeo-Christian biblical tradition and more especially in the spiritual tradition of the East is never to be reduced to what concerns affectivity or the feelings.

In the Bible, the heart is the vital core of the human personality. It is the part we sometimes call the soul, the inmost depth of our being. It is the all-important area where integration takes place, where all our human faculties, life-processes and bodily functions are based, converge, harmonise.

The heart is that place especially where each of us is near God, can communicate with him who is the source of life. It is the field Jesus spoke about where the treasure of the kingdom of heaven lies hid (cf Mt 13:44).

'The heart indeed is the master and king of the whole physical organism and when grace takes over the pastures of the heart it reigns over all the members and all the thoughts, for true intelligence is there...' (St Macarius).

And throughout religious history how many men and women have entered into the silence of the heart, at that fine point of their being where they glimpse another dimension of themselves and of the world. Silence introduces them to a world they have not made, which was there already in them, but as though buried. Then one day they become conscious of it.

The heart or the soul is without a doubt the most beautiful and hidden of the Creator's gifts to his creatures.

So every person, atheist or believer, possesses this inner faculty, capable of entering into relations with God since he has breathed his own Spirit there. In the silence of the soul it is no longer we who take the initiative but God, whose Spirit is joined to our spirit. There is no longer a private soliloquy but a listening to a divine word, inexpressible like the murmur of a spring. There, just as the sap rises and spreads silently through the tree, the Creator Spirit touched the hearts of his creatures with small, scarcely discernible touches which only a silent person can perceive.

15

Learn to be at home
in the heart

The tragedy of modern people is that having deserted the heart they do not even know they possess an interior life. The result is they have a fear of silence, which they confuse with emptiness. They have lost the way to the heart for a variety of reasons, psychological, social and cultural, which were sketched out at the beginning of this work. The path still exists but it is as though covered with undergrowth like a winding footpath no longer in use which ends by disappearing under brambles.

Many men and women have never really been conscious of this inner treasure quite simply because no one had shown them how to 'dwell in the heart', how to experience silence at this level of their being. And just as any unused faculty – physical or intellectual – will atrophy, so this inner faculty has ended in sclerosis.

To all these reasons should probably also be added a profound misconception of the God of Jesus Christ, often reduced to a caricature. We cannot find the way to the heart again and the taste for silence except at the price of a twofold purification, of our understanding of God and our conception of humanity.

Who wants to enter into dialogue with a distant God, vague and impersonal on the model of Voltaire's Great Clockmaker or some cold lawgiver? Dialogue is not possible with an abstract Being we can't very well see taking any interest in our everyday life.

There would be no joy in silent loving intimacy with a utilitarian stop-gap God, to be at our service when things go wrong. I would have no desire to meet a God who set my freedom aside by purely arbitrary external commands...

No silent inner dialogue or happy relations are possible with such a caricature of God and human beings. And if God is denied or rejected, the human being is left alone and the silence is nothing but a barren confrontation with oneself, one's radical precariousness and anxiety before the void, our only outlook for the future.

Modern people also ask how silence can be indwelt by God, can be a place for intimate dialogue. St Paul has already answered this query by affirming that it is possible, for the simple reason that God himself has taken the initiative and given us the means.

'The Spirit helps us in our weakness, for we do not know how to pray as we ought, but that very Spirit intercedes with sighs too deep for words. And God who searches the heart knows what is in the mind of the Spirit' (Rom 8:26-27).

To keep silence is a way of preparing our heart to welcome the 'mind of the Spirit' within us. Christian prayer springs up in silence not primarily from a need or out of fear of other human beings but from an inner call of the Spirit. Prayer is rooted in the initiative by the God of Love who wishes to fill us with his Presence.

16

Only a silence inhabited by Love is for our good

How can we dare enter into silence, persevering in prayer, if we are not convinced of being 'indwelt' by the Spirit who is the mind of God in us? A God who reveals himself as the power of creative Love who humanises, personalises, divinises human beings. A God whose love does not set aside our liberty but liberates us, forms us, creates us by loving us.

It is true that left to ourselves we are terribly earthbound, earthy, terrestrial. There is a solidity natural to us which inclines us to what is palpable, visible, sensible. St Paul has already made this clear by comparing the physical and the spiritual.

'For what human being knows what is truly human except the human spirit that is within?' Indeed the human sciences are increasingly advancing in understanding of our human psychological mechanisms. But, adds St Paul at once: 'No one comprehends what is truly God's except the Spirit of God', the Spirit which comes from God and which we receive (1 Cor 2:10-16).

The inner, spiritual dimension of the world, of reality, is not familiar to us. But, writes St Paul again: 'God has sent the Spirit of his Son into our hearts, crying: Abba! Father!' (Gal 4:6).

And how could we hear the murmuring of this inner spring of the Spirit in our heart unless we keep silence which too is a gift of God.

So the silence of the heart is much more than a matter of surroundings or a psychological phenomenon. It is a manifestation of the breathing of the Spirit in us who sighs to God, adores and intercedes. I do not 'keep' silence: I enter into it. I open myself to a Presence who makes words unnecessary. This 'spiritual' silence we do not obtain for ourselves: it is given.

This silence is out of reach of relaxing exercises, physical or mental. It is not enough to unwind physically or even psychologically in order to enter into the silence of God. The gushing fountain of the Spirit has to be set free in us.

God is present everywhere, in the city as much as in the desert, but it is in the silence of the heart that we learn to discern that Presence, hear his light step in each passing day. 'I did not say: "Seek me in chaos"' (Is 45:19).

The whole of the Bible, essentially a centuries long apprenticeship in the dialogue between God and the human race, culminates in this verse from St John: 'Those who love me will keep my word, and my Father will love them, and we will come to them and make our home with them' (Jn 14:23). And this 'home' is our heart where we can henceforth, as Christ says: 'Worship the Father in spirit and in truth.'

St Paul writes: 'I pray that you may be strengthened in your inner being with power through his Spirit, and that Christ may dwell in your hearts through faith, as you are being rooted and grounded in love' (Eph 3:16ff). He, the zealous Pharisee with such respect for the Temple, transported by the Christian revelation can boldly say to his brethren: 'Do you not know that you are God's temple – the Holy of Holies – and that God's Spirit dwells in you? God's temple is holy and you are that temple' (1 Cor 3:16-17).

Dazzled on the road to Damascus by the Risen Christ he understands that all the temples at Delphi, Athens and even Jerusalem, are nothing but signs of this new reality. From now on anyone who enters into the silence of the heart can hear the murmur of God's voice, receive the Spirit of the living Christ, and so share in the eternal dialogue of Father and Son.

What a revelation is this! It illumines the whole history of creation and human destiny. No, a human being is not a gut open at both ends. No, the human being is not a mass of flesh, particles and cells. No, we are not the result of chance. No, humans are not only animals born to feed, reproduce and die. A human being is created to become the silent dwelling of God, Father, Son, and Holy Spirit.

That is the summit of the Judeo-Christian revelation, where all the groping search for dialogue with the divinity in all the great religions achieves its end.

So to keep silence is to dwell in the house of our heart where God is always there before us. To keep silence is to be present to that eternal spiritual presence of God.

I do not have to create it by pious or fervid auto-suggestion but to receive it in the silence of faith.

To speak of a spiritual presence does not mean calling up an imaginary unreal presence. Revelation shows us indeed that the real surpasses the sensible or the visible. To keep silence is to be continually reborn to our identity through our own hidden depths: 'What is born of the flesh is flesh, and what is born of the Spirit is spirit. Do not be astonished that I said to you, "You must be born from above." The wind blows where it chooses, and you hear the sound of it, but you do not know where it comes from or where it goes. So it is with everyone who is born of the Spirit' (Jn 3:6-8).

How will anyone be able to live with their actions,

words, relationships, silences without dwelling in the heart? Here at the end of this chapter we are in a better position to gauge the paradox of modern people, who are able to explore the planets, the moon and the stars, to analyse the intricacies of the brain, sound the ocean depths, control the amazing mechanisms of life, push back the frontiers of death... and who have lost the way to their own heart.

We no longer know ourselves. Anguished rather than marvelling at our own mystery we wander about like children showered with gifts but no longer knowing the way home. We have become strangers to ourselves, exiles from our native land.

Knowing how to dwell in silence is the secret of happiness. It is in the heart that we learn to love, to marvel at being alive, each one a single note fleeting but necessary in the symphony of life. How can we love others if we do not love ourselves as a result of finding ourselves wholly loved by the Creator?

Happy the one who can find the way to that interior garden where at the evening air will perhaps be heard the echo of a gentle voice: 'Adam, where are you?' Mysterious Presence supporting our venture and constituting our greatness. One who does not love will find silence unbearable. One who loves will transform silence into intimacy. The love of silence leads to the silence of Love.

17

Silence:
crucible of a new person

The Christian revelation provides another estimation of why we find it so difficult to live at ease in the heart, to know this happiness, this intimate conversation with God. It is the tragedy of what is traditionally called sin, that mysterious breach between the human race and God.

'The man and the woman heard the sound of the Lord God walking in the garden at the time of the evening breeze, and the man and his wife hid themselves from the presence of the Lord God among the trees of the garden. But the Lord God called to the man, and said to him, "Where are you?".' This inspired dialogue written during the exile following the taking of Jerusalem perfectly symbolises this difficulty of encounter between the Creator and his creatures after the Fall. The human race has become that paradoxical being with aspirations to happiness and fullness of life who at the same time flees from the One who alone can provide what is sought.

Human beings have used their freedom to claim absolute autonomy, at the risk of becoming closed to the appeal of God's love which is the basis and guarantee of that fragile liberty. The human heart originally went out toward God the source of its being, development and end but has become as it were turned in on itself. The desire for happiness, according to the mind of the Spirit, has splintered into a thousand desires more or less narrow or illusory.

Since that mysterious break with God our heart itself, as St Paul says, has become senseless, dull, darkened. 'They became futile in their thinking, and their senseless minds were darkened. Claiming to be wise, they became fools; and they exchanged the glory of God for idols' (Rom 1:21-23). Out of egoism or pride we make ourselves the centre, the sole object of our desiring.

Slaves to fragmented desires scattered in all directions where happiness is nowhere to be found, we destroy ourselves by refusing Life. Sin is nothing but a perversion of the desire for happiness, a deviant of our desire to love and be loved, a turning back of human desire onto self, idolatry. Sin is the desire for happiness which has lost its way.

One who knows how to find the way back to the heart, to listen to the mind of the Spirit, finds by experience that, gradually, these desires are not denied nor frustrated but purified, redirected, made simple.

Silence becomes a place for conversion, where we pass from the narcissistic being centred on self to openness to God and to others who are desired and loved for themselves.

By turning away from God the human race brought about the 'fall', one of its serious consequences being loss of integrity. Being shut out from the heart meant poor communication between that 'inward faculty' and the other faculties such as intelligence and will.

This starts up a crisis of identity to the extent that there is a dichotomy between what we really are fundamentally, beings created 'in the image and likeness of God', and what we think we are, as we conceive ourselves in the mind.

One who learns to dwell in the silence of the heart, to welcome the Spirit, will discover the extent to which that spiritual energy of fruitful, productive Love progressively integrates all the faculties, unifies the whole being. It opens up new ways of knowing, the way of spiritual understanding and a new way of loving: charity, love in the Spirit. In the end, the quality of our relationships, our actions, our daily existence, depends on how we live in the heart, where the Kingdom is already present.

More and more psychologists are giving as much attention to meditation as to furthering relationships, the interaction between the two appearing increasingly evident to them. They willingly accept that the silence of meditation greatly influences the quality of our relationships and personal intimacy.

It does indeed take a great deal of silence for us to leave our possessive love which loves itself in others, for a detached love which loves others for themselves. The philosopher Lévinas, while continuing to defend the rights others have on us, affirms that only those beings which have been able to maintain a real relation with solitude are in a position to relate to others.

In the main the great religions hold silence to be a place of purification. The wisdom of the Buddha even sees in it an indispensable teacher of detachment from all desire, the source of illusions which deflect us from the world's true reality.

The Christian tradition, as we have seen, attributes to silence a quite different end. While silent meditation allows us to examine and purify all the successive layers of our psyche, conscious or unconscious, we believe that only the Spirit is the source of that new inner freedom which will favour authentic intimacy with God and with others.

This inner detachment prepares us for an intuitive knowledge of the Other and of others: the heart's knowledge transcending thoughts, images and words. This knowledge is a fruit of love which opens us to what the Christian tradition calls the indwelling of God in us, one of the great themes of the Gospel of St John, where Jesus says explicitly: 'On that day you will know that I am in my Father and you in me, and I in you' (Jn 14:20). Indwelling is intimate love without fusion of those loving, as it is in the mystery of the triune God who is total unity and total alterity.

There is a depth of feeling contained in that other text of St John: 'Listen, I am standing at the door and knocking; if you hear my voice and open the door, I will come in to you and eat with you and you with me' (Rev 3:20). We are free to accept or refuse this intimacy with God inviting us. Silence is without doubt the best way to put oneself in the state of mind to hear the voice within of the one knocking at the door of our heart, and open to him.

In the silence of meditation we accustom ourselves to this union which is differential, this loving communion which is not absorption into a great cosmic whole, but one in which we each become more ourselves.

Without this opportunity to love – which unites us in respect for each one – every human relationship, all intimacy between husband and wife, parents and children, or between friends, will be more difficult. Only the Spirit of love purifies us in silence and detaches us from any desire of appropriating others to achieve closer union. To this interior purification might be applied the beautiful parable of Jesus inviting us to sell, lose, all joyfully in order to acquire the treasure buried in our heart and in the heart of others: true love (cf Mt 13:4).

18

Jesus and silence

In the New Testament there are only brief allusions to silence: the silence Jesus imposed on the sea and on demons, or the embarrassed silence of his enemies and his disciples disconcerted by his questions. St Paul asks the faithful in their meetings to balance freedom to speak with fraternal silence (cf 1 Cor 14:28-34).

But while not being explicitly mentioned, silence still has an important place in the life and mission of the man Jesus. He thus reveals to us its true dimension beyond any human wisdom.

Let us simply recall the fact, so rich in implication for our personal life and the mission of the whole Church, that he, Jesus, the Word of God made flesh, the Father's envoy, the missionary par excellence, began by remaining silent for thirty years. Love incarnate in the course of daily life does not need to make a lot of noise.

A more beautiful recognition of the value and fruitfulness of silence, made humbly present in solidarity with human life and work, is not to be imagined. The silence of Nazareth which fascinated Charles de Foucauld, for example, is a compelling word revealing the mystery of God among us.

And in the course of his short public ministry, entirely given over to proclaiming the Kingdom of God, Jesus again manifests the essential role of silence in the life of every disciple. It is not by chance that St Mark at the beginning of his gospel includes in Jesus' typical missionary day a time of silence: 'In the morning, while it was still very dark, he got up and went out to a deserted place and there he prayed' (Mk 1:35ff).

Mark aims to show his readers that prayer in solitude is not for Jesus an occasional aside but an essential part of his being and his mission. Jesus does not seek out silence for itself but rather in order to hold filial converse with the One dwelling in his heart, his thoughts and actions, his prayer, and by whom he is sent: God, his Father.

The evangelist seeks to demonstrate to the Christian community how the source of Jesus' mission, the dynamism of his commitment, the implanting of the Good News, are from God, received, loved and heard in silence.

Simon sets off after him with his companions. And when they find him they say to him: 'Everyone is looking for you.' Jesus does not allow himself to be overwhelmed by the demand, the popularity, the number of the sick. His times of silence in the presence of the Father are as vital to him as the air he breathes. He will never oppose action to contemplation. Love requires a two-fold outgoing, to his Father and to people. In the silence of prayer he lays himself open to the Father and his loving design.

And the evangelists have kept for us traces of this duality solitude/presence to people, silence/word which regulates his whole public life. After the multiplication of the loaves, 'When Jesus realised that they were about to come and take him by force to make him king, he withdrew again to the mountain by himself' (Jn 6:15). 'Now more than ever the word about Jesus spread abroad; many crowds would gather to hear and to be cured of their diseases. But he would withdraw to deserted places and pray' (Lk 5:15-16).

We know how people always try to claim God on their side for their projects, their ideologies, their wars. So, in front of the dubious enthusiasm of the crowds always attracted by a reductionist messianism, bound by their earthly concerns, Jesus is a man of separation and communion. A separation necessary in order the better to live in authentic solidarity with human beings in accordance with his Father's will, which so far surpasses our limited horizons. The silence of prayer is indispensable for him to continue his mission in its purity and to respond to its demands.

To his disciples who come looking for him in his solitude Jesus replies: '"Let us go on to the neighbouring towns, so that I may proclaim the message; for that is what I came out to do." And he went on throughout Galilee proclaiming the message in their synagogues and casting out demons' (Mk 1:38-39). So this silence is in no way an escape or a 'flight from the world' but a time for strengthening which allows Jesus to go on further.

If silence is often for him an occasion for showing genuine filial love, sometimes it is also a necessary time of reflection before taking important decisions concerning his mission; before choosing his first disciples, for example: 'Now during those days he went out to the mountain to pray; and he spent the night in prayer to God. And when day came he called his disciples and chose twelve of them' (Lk 6:12-13).

19

God said all
when he died in silence

If Christ's silences are words as important as the teaching he left to us, the most eloquent silence in the New Testament is that of Jesus during his trial. He feared neither to denounce the hypocrisy of the Pharisees nor to confront the Father of Lies, but he is silent before the High Priest (Mk 14:61), Herod (Lk 23:9) and Pilate (Mk 15:5). Silence of the Just One which contrasts with the unjust attitude of aggression in his adversaries. Dignified silence of the Messiah whose 'hour' has now come and whose only power is the strength radiating from truth.

'When he was accused by the chief priests and elders, he did not answer. Then Pilate said to him, "Do you not hear how many accusations they make against you?" But he gave them no answer, not even to a single charge, so that the governor was greatly amazed' (Mt 27:12-14).

But never is his silence cowardice. When truth demands he does not hesitate to speak out clearly. Rising, the High Priest said to him: "'I put you under oath before the living God, tell us if you are the Messiah, the Son of God." Jesus said to him, "You have said so"' (Mt 26:63-64).

Though Christ does speak some words on the cross there is mostly silence. The silence of this crucified man becomes a searing shattering word. God said everything when he died in silence.

If human silence seems to be more highly valued in the Old Testament judging by the abundance of examples, it should be noted that the texts in the New Testament have additional light thrown on them from the fact of referring to the person of Jesus Christ. The silence surrounding the mystery of Jesus does not fail to evoke the very mystery enveloping God. It is no longer the silence of simple human wisdom but attains the level of theology.

20

Come yourselves
into a desert place apart

On their return from the first apostolic journey, Jesus said to his apostles: 'Come away to a deserted place all by yourselves and rest a while' (Mk 6:31). The wisdom and solicitude of Christ who knows that his men need to take a break for reflection on the results good and bad of their mission, to be with him, to report back and enjoy a well-earned rest in his company. The more the envoy is immersed in human company the greater the need to build up strength again in the presence of the Master. Here Mark sketches the constant rhythm of any missionary life: reception of the Lord's word in silence along with public proclamation, contemplation along with apostolic labours.

This is not to forget that the word 'rest' has a particular biblical resonance. To enter into God's rest meant entering the Promised Land, the place where he was to dwell with his people. For Mark, this rest evokes the new intimacy with Christ, God among us. As St John says admirably, every Christian is a witness to a Presence heard and contemplated in the silence of prayer (cf 1 Jn 1:1ff)

And when in the face of adversity the witness is tempted to flee, it is again in silence that will be heard afresh the voice of the One sending and there will be new courage to continue the mission. The attempt at 'demission' by the prophet Elijah is a profound illustration of this (cf 1 Kings 19:1-15).

Elijah has just triumphed over the false prophets in the service of the cruel idolatrous Queen Jezebel. Enraged she lets him know she will have him put to death at the first opportunity.

Terror stricken, Elijah flees into the desert: 'He was afraid; he got up and fled for his life, and came to Beersheba, which belongs to Judah; he left his servant there.' The fiery prophet so sure of being invested with the power of his God is no more than a poor man seized with physical fear. He is at the end of his tether. He takes refuge in the desert, fully determined to make off unknown into the wilds.

'But he himself went a day's journey into the wilderness, and came and sat down under a solitary broom tree. He asked that he might die: "It is enough; now, O Lord, take away my life, for I am no better than my ancestors." Then he lay down under the broom tree and fell asleep.'

He is overwhelmed by the disproportion between the weight of his mission and his human capacity. The first hours of his solitary march are mostly taken up with himself, his problems, his failure. Time will be needed for him to calm his raging thoughts, his questionings, his rebelliousness, still tumultuous even in the silence of the desert, which only amplifies his inner turmoil. Only one refuge remains to him, sleep. To sleep, to forget. Think about nothing. Sleep too is sometimes a form of escape.

'Suddenly an angel touched him and said to him, "Get up and eat." He looked, and there at his head was a cake baked on hot stones, and a jar of water. He ate and drank, and lay down again. The angel of the Lord came a second time, touched him and said, "Get up and eat, otherwise the journey will be too much for you." He got up, and ate and drank.'

God does not abandon his servant. Twice he gently visits him, brings him out of his torpor, a symbol of all our spiritual weariness, and makes him eat. Elijah had to build up his strength, for his inner journey had only just begun. To do so he must in silence receive God's gifts, eat the bread of his Word and drink the living water of the Spirit.

'Then he went in the strength of that food forty days and forty nights to Horeb the mount of God.' Elijah has symbolically to follow the faith-journey of his people, retrace the way to Mount Sinai, the special place of meeting. It was there God sealed a covenant with humankind, there that the Exodus venture took on full significance, there that he revealed his 'name' to Moses. Elijah had to strengthen his vocation afresh by a personal experience of the presence of God, of the One who sent him, and found his mission anew on God's loving design in salvation history. A very personal experience, indescribable, which the biblical author symbolises by the superb image of silence like a breath of air.

'At that place he came to a cave, and spent the night there. Then the word of the Lord came to him, saying, "What are you doing here, Elijah?" He answered, "I have been very zealous for the Lord, the God of hosts; for the Israelites have forsaken your covenant, thrown down your altars, and killed your prophets with the sword. I alone am left and they are seeking my life, to take it away."' Elijah begins with a cry of discouragement. His passion for God's cause is not dead and it is for that very reason that he is hurt by God's apparent failure in face of the hostility, the indifference of the impious, and the desertion of the people, unfaithful to the covenant.

A voice said to him: 'Go out and stand on the mountain before the Lord.' This cave at the mouth of which Elijah is standing also recalls the symbol of the heart at the entrance to which each must stand in order to sense the quiet passing of God.

The Lord was about to pass by. 'Now there was a great wind, so strong that it was splitting mountains and breaking rocks in pieces before the Lord, but the Lord was not in the wind, and after the wind an earthquake, but the Lord was not in the earthquake, and after the earthquake a fire, but the Lord was not in the fire; and after the fire a sound of sheer silence.'

Elijah no doubt was looking for a spectacular 'theophany', a grandiose manifestation of God. He was still putting his hope in a strong God, capable of triumphing over his adversaries. The Lord undertook to purify his too human conceptions which projected his own desire for domination or violence.

God was neither in the clamour of the storm nor in the fury of the earthquake, writes the inspired author. God came to Elijah in the nothing of a slight breath of air, the murmuring of a light breeze which can only be heard in silence. 'Elijah heard it.'

He discovers that God is present as a whisper, a stir, a breath of life like that spoken of in the Book of Genesis where it says that 'God breathed the breath of life' to make Adam into a living being (Gen 2:7).

'The Lord said to him, "Go, return on your way…".' Fortified anew by this spiritual experience, this intimacy with God found again in silence, Elijah is from now on capable of hearing God's call afresh and starting out again to accomplish his mission. In his heart resounds anew: 'Go', the command which makes witnesses and prophets. He has revived his inner courage based on the conviction that his battle is the Lord's and that he will never leave him alone. He had to go through the stripping and silence of the desert to find again the wellspring of his vocation and God's free gift of salvation.

People of silence

'A saint ripens in silence' (Georges Bernanos).

Indeed God manifestly gives a continuous teaching course. He always begins by sending those to whom he wishes to confide a service for his people 'into the desert': Moses to the desert of Midian, John the Baptist to the desert of Judea, St Paul to the Syrian desert, St Benedict to the mountain solitudes of Subiaco, St Ignatius Loyola to Manresa, St Francis of Assisi to the caves in the countryside near Assisi.

A truth time, when the person admits to being poor, and is open to God's gifts. A time of rooting in faith. A necessary time for breaking away in order to receive a new freedom and to prepare for living a new communion with all people. All the great witnesses in salvation history were to remain lovers of silence in spite of an often very active life.

They could not be called witnesses to Christ if they did not relive in one form or another his own example of missionary life, with its alternating rhythm of adoration of the Father and service of humanity. Anyone with no taste for silence risks aping religion as a functionary of the sacred, not a collaborator with God.

'For you, Lord, even silence is praise, says the psalmist (Ps 64 in the Greek version). And so: from the first hermits in the desert to the monks and nuns of today, thousands of men and women have shown their predilection for solitude, not for its own sake but in order to seek God there.

St Bernard saw in it symbolically a second purificatory baptism: 'This monk has been buried again with Christ by the baptism of the desert.'

They have in particular been fascinated by an adaptation of the well-known text from the Prophet Hosea often to be found written over the entrance to the cloister: 'I will draw you and lead you into the desert and there speak to your heart.' They have always held solitude to be the place required for loving intimacy with God, so as to be open to his presence.

Charles de Foucauld wrote: It is necessary to go into the desert and stay there in order to receive God's grace – this desert is profoundly sweet to me: it is so sweet and good to feel oneself alone before the eternal. One feels invaded by truth. So it is hard for me to have to go about and leave the solitude and silence.

The link between solitude and silence is deeply rooted in the centuries-old tradition of the spiritual life in all the religions. But as we have seen, solitude is not a foregone conclusion. Bernanos, again, wrote that hell too has its cloisters. The Desert Fathers have said enough about their combat and phantasms to make us see that a prolonged stay in solitude is no easy option.

Solitude can even have disastrous effects for some temperaments, the nervous or the sensitive, and also as much on the physical as on the supernatural plane. It is not possible to go from an active life straight into the desert, far from any direct contact, without feeling a kind of desiccating impoverishment and being plunged into the ambivalent world of the imagination and the various classic compensatory mechanisms.

So solitude is no ideal place for all and on all occasions. The first evidence of this is that anyone aspiring to solitude with a self-seeking purpose or for show will not stay long.

There are many rooms in God's house and many ways of getting there. So prolonged solitude is not the only way to God. On the other hand no one can entirely do without proper times of silence and solitude.

Solitude can take different forms. And the Lord grants to each the type of silence which is most appropriate. There are times in our life when it is more suitable and necessary than others. The length of time and the frequency are a matter for human spiritual discernment which requires on-going counsel from an accredited spiritual adviser.

God's graces and calls are not all alike. Not everyone is called to be a hermit in the desert or a Cistercian or a Carthusian. In the end as we have already suggested every vocation, however solitary, always implies a mission. Beginning with Abraham, the call of the Covenant God, though made to an individual, is always directed to the salvation and the future of the People of God. Voillaume for example says in regard to Charles de Foucauld: 'His vocation was indeed a vocation to be present among people, a presence intended as a witness to Christ's love.'

The paradox is only apparent, for we learn by experience that we can be very close in mind and heart to those who are far away, and very distant in the midst of a crowd. Proximity is not to be confused with presence. It is not necessary to be close to our next-door neighbour for them to be aware of us. St Thérèse of Lisieux was named patron of the missions without ever having left her Carmel. There she used to say: 'I shall be love so I shall be all.'

It is this quality of ardent heart-felt love which turns isolation or mere proximity into true presence.

The best way is the one God wants for us, the one indicated by circumstances or imposed by temperament; in the end, the one where we can love God and others better.

22

Silence
a school for seeing

Love silence.
Let it school you. It will be your teacher.
It will show you how to see the icon which is Jesus
Christ,
it will show you how to accustom the eyes of your
heart
to the face of God
revealed in your own and in the face of humanity.

Love silence.
Let it school you. It will be your teacher.
It will show you how to see the disfigured face of
Jesus Christ.
It will show you how to accustom the eyes of your
heart
to the face of God
looking at you through the eyes of the victims of
starvation and torture.

Love silence.
Let it school you. It will be your teacher.
It will show you how to see the transfigured face of
Jesus Christ.
It will show you how to accustom the eyes of your
heart
to discern at the heart of creation

reflections of the heart of the Creator,
to discern in the opacity of things and of other beings
their true dimension
and in the humble actions of every created being
traces of his goodness.

Love silence.
Let it school you. It will be your teacher.
It will show you how to see the face of Jesus Christ,
human and divine,
origin and consummation of our history.
It will show you how to accustom the eyes of your
heart
to see the gleams of light at the end of the tunnel,
the seeds of eternity in the fleeting present,
and the still hidden future of every living being.

Love silence.
Let it school you. It will be your teacher
It will show you how to see the true face of humanity
and of God,
it will give you inner eyes of faith
which shows us how to see people,
their joys and sufferings,
their hopes and despairing,
all the big and little events of life,
with the eyes of Jesus Christ.

23

Silence and speech

Silence in no way differs from inner speech (L. Lavelle).

At the basic level silence opens us to the voice of our own consciousness. What in effect would thought be without words to express it? In the same way silence with no inward speech would be only an acoustic void. And on a higher level silence opens us to the Word of God which touches our heart with the words of Christ and the inspiration of the Spirit.

Silence is not, then, the absence or denial of speech but on the contrary acceptance of every interior word in which every exterior word should be rooted. 'Souls float in silence as gold floats in distilled water, and the words we speak have no meaning without the silence which bathes them' (Maeterlinck).

If speech is not as it were wrapped or interspersed by silence it becomes an avalanche of words, and music a cacophony of sounds. Without silence before and after, human speech and music would be no more than an unbearable succession of uninterrupted sound. Silence gives each word and musical note their proper density and colour.

So it is not by chance that in the biblical tradition silence precedes or prolongs the Word, illuminating after its fashion the dialogue between God and humanity. The scenes of theophany or manifestation of God are often as it were enveloped in a vast and reverent silence.

'The Lord is in his holy temple; let all the earth keep silence before him' (Hab 2:20).

And the announcement of one of God's interventions in favour of his people is often joined by an invitation to adopt an attitude of silence:

Be silent before the Lord God!
For the Day of the Lord is at hand (Zeph 1:7).
Listen to me in silence, O coastlands;
let the people renew their strength;
let them approach, then let them speak;
let us together draw near for judgment (Is 41:1).
Be silent, all people, before the Lord,
for he has roused himself from his holy dwelling
(Zech 2:13).
When the Lamb opened the seventh seal, there was silence
in heaven for about half an hour (Rev 8:1).

As St John writes in his marvellous Prologue, in the beginning was the Word and the Word was God and that word was as though wrapped in a pregnant silence. 'For while gentle silence enveloped all things, and night in its swift course was now half gone, your all-powerful word leaped from heaven from the royal throne' (Wis 18:14-15).

Regarding Christ's Incarnation, St Paul speaks of a revelation, a mystery kept in silence through eternal ages but now made manifest and brought to the knowledge of all the peoples (Rom 16:25).

Silence envelops and precedes the revealed Word. Today as yesterday the Word cannot be born in human hearts and in humanity as a whole except through a long, sweet, secret maturation, the mystical silence of divine creative love.

24

Listening silence

If the God of the Bible speaks to his people we can understand that listening is the characteristic of the Judeo-Christian tradition.

Moses says, 'Keep silence and listen, O Israel. This very day you have become the people of the Lord your God. Therefore listen to the voice of the Lord God and you will keep his commandments' (cf Deut 27:9).

But for the people in the Bible the word of God does not fall from heaven like a meteor or a voice from the wings. It is born at the conjunction of events and those who experience them. The conjunction of an historical event in the life of the people (exodus from Egypt, exile to Babylon) and the one who, inspired by the Spirit of God, interprets that event.

Inseparable in the biblical concept of 'People of God' are the history of a people and the message delivered by those with an authentic spiritual experience (inspiration).

All through history God raises up 'mediators' – Abraham, Moses, prophets, sages – who in the silence of the desert or of the heart listen to the Spirit, reflect on and interpret the profound significance of their people's history and see there a Presence acting, God. These events then become words of God, intelligible messages to transmit to all the people.

In the same line of thought, in St John for example, the verb to listen or to hear is very important. It recurs 58 times in his Gospel, 16 times in his Letters, and 46 times in Revelation. It is part of the vocabulary of revelation, 22 times referring to Jesus, his person, his needs or his voice, and 4 times to the Father or the voice of the Father.

Jesus, a lover of silence as we have seen, presents himself as the one who says, reveals, attests, what he has himself heard. He lives constantly listening out for the Father. He is 'the one who comes from above... He testifies to what he has seen and heard' (Jn 3:31-32). 'The one who sent me is true and I declare to the world what I have heard from him' (8:26).

And the Jews want to kill him because he says, reveals, the truth to them. 'Now you are trying to kill me, a man who has told you the truth that I have heard from the Father' (8:40).

He is the Son who makes known to his disciples as friends all that he has heard from the Father. 'I have made known to you everything that I have heard from the Father' (15:15).

The disciple, after the example of Jesus, is one who listens. The adventure in faith of following Jesus always begins with a word heard. Thus it is on hearing the word of their master that two of the Baptist's disciples set off to follow Jesus. But the word of Jesus himself is yet more penetrating.

That is what the Samaritans announce after hearing the woman's witness on her return from the well. 'Many more believed because of his word. They said to the woman, "It is no longer because of what you said that we believe, for we have heard for ourselves, and we know that this is truly so"' (4:41-42).

If the woman's word awakened their faith, the word of Jesus heard and listened to has transformed their incipient faith into a personal conviction: That man is the Saviour. Hearing is an essential part of faith.

In John there is a very close link between hearing and believing. 'Anyone who hears my word and believes in him who sent me has eternal life' (5:24). To listen to the word of Jesus, recognise in it that of God's envoy and believe it, hold to it as to the Word of the Father himself, constitute a single act. Now this hearing and believing requires certain inner dispositions, an essential being acceptance and reflection in the silence of our heart.

Thus listening is not the fruit of empty discussion but of 'listening silence' which itself is by an action on the part of God who inclines the human heart to open to his revelation. 'No one can come to me unless drawn by the Father who sent me; and I will raise that person up on the last day. It is written, "And they shall all be taught by God." Everyone who has heard and learned from the Father comes to me' (6:44-45).

Another related theme in John is that of 'hearing the voice', which implies a more direct connection with the person of Jesus himself: his is the voice of the Son of God (5:25), of the Son of Man, judge of the living and the dead (5:27-29), the Shepherd (10:3-5; 16-27), king and witness to the truth (18:37).

As compared to the word, the voice has the stronger connotation of a call, a pressing invitation. At the voice of the Master calling her, Mary gets up in haste and comes to Jesus (11:28-29). To hear and especially to listen to the voice suppose a mutual attachment between the one issuing the call and the one who receives it.

The Good Shepherd discourse (Jn 18) is very enlightening and shows well the shade of intimacy implied by listening to the voice. The sheep 'hear his voice' because each one is called by name and they recognise the Shepherd's voice. Like Mary of Magdala who recognised the voice of her Lord on simply hearing her name 'Mary!' Like the bride in the Song of Songs who recognises the voice of the beloved (2:8; 5:2; 8:13). Mary recognises him not by sight (since she took him for the gardener) but by his voice, by hearing.

It is the same for John the Baptist. He compares himself to the friend of the bridegroom who 'stands and hears him, rejoices greatly at the bridegroom's voice' (3:29).

God's word cannot touch the heart except of one who is prepared and in a listening state. Only one who is a seeker after God, a lover of silence listening out for God, can hear him.

25

Silence has its battles

It would not be honest to make it appear that silence is always an easy path, one well marked out, to the heart at rest, and a meeting with God. Silence is also a place of sometimes fearsome combat against obstacles, the forces of evil in its many forms. Whether we call it sin, the devil or darkness matters little. One thing is sure: it is impossible to set out on the paths of silence without some day coming up against a combat as exemplified by the agony at Gethsemane.

Luke has summed up for us in a few verses a grievous inner conflict which may have lasted for hours. A conflict in which Jesus knew the daunting solitude of a man abandoned by all, the profoundly human sense of anguish. 'In his anguish, he prayed more earnestly' (Lk 22:28-46). Is there anyone who has never experienced in some degree that anguished loneliness which grips what is vital in us, enfeebles our thinking, when we are faced with a health problem, failure, an abrupt end to hopes for the future?

Jesus takes on this human situation where silence is no longer a sweet filial intimacy but a cry of revolt. The shocking silence of the absence of God. A cry unechoed in the black night. During this combat (*agonia* means combat), Jesus goes on praying to his Father but his acceptance is slow and lacerating. He is showing how difficult it is for a human being to pass from human projects to the unfathomable designs of God.

Gradually Jesus goes from revolt, gut fear, refusal, to trust. The efficaciousness of this long prayer of conflict before God's silence is not what we would humanly have expected. For Jesus is not to be dispensed from confronting the forces of evil, suffering, his passion and death. But when the soldiers come to arrest him he has unquestionably recovered the inner peace and strength to live through these sorrowful events. It is on this level that his prayer is heard. It will resound in the triumph of life on the day of his raising from the dead by the Father.

Since the first hermits the Christian tradition has always held the solitude of the desert to be a privileged place of meeting with God but also a place for confronting the forces of evil.

In the fourth century St Anthony, often called the Father of monasticism, was driven by the Spirit to the silence of the sandy desert between the Nile and the Red Sea where he had to measure up to the Devil, the Father of Lies.

So this 'going out into the desert' (anachoresis) is never an escape, a flight from the difficulties of daily life, but quite the contrary a call to fight with the Enemy. This redemptive combat is only possible if closely lived 'with Christ'.

The solitary, far from being anti-social, is conscious of living in communion with the People of God and of fighting in the name of the whole Church against the forces of evil ceaselessly threatening the world. So this going into retreat involves much more than the one individual. The monk is part of the vast confrontation between light and darkness, good and evil.

It is this which explains the important place often given in the 'Lives', as for example of St Anthony, to diabolical appearances which sometimes make us smile.

But it is for us to discern the theological and mystical import of the combat.

In times of trial, sometimes, in order to avoid mortal attacks of evil or despair we must contemplate in silence the cross of Christ who knew 'the silence of God'; Christ, the new Moses, who passed through the desert of evil and the waters of death to enter into the Father's Kingdom and take us with him in his train, the Easter triumph which gives meaning to all our 'desert combats'.

26

Christ's temptations
in the desert

These temptations recapitulate and symbolise those of every individual and of human civilisation as whole. In the silence of the desert Jesus had to take on and surmount three intimately connected snares or temptations which derive from three basic, legitimate needs inherent in our very human nature: the need to possess, to be of consequence and to have power.

'If you are the Son of God, command these stones to become bread' (cf Mt 4:1-11). Jesus too experienced this primary human need: the need of bread to live. The vital primary, elemental hunger soon becomes a legitimate need to possess in order to secure guarantees for the future. It is then that the temptation or snare arises: to amass capital for an excessive degree of well-being, to hoard goods and wealth, to rest content with satisfying our earthly appetites, to safeguard our immediate needs. This is a temptation which ends by stifling any sense of generosity and sharing, all openness to the heart's riches, to human relationships and God's gifts.

Our Western society further exacerbates this instinctive fixation on the need to possess. Jesus unmasked the tragic illusion. He, the incarnate Bread of the Word, Bread of life, knows that the transcendent fullness of God is alone capable of stilling our hunger for the absolute. Humanity does not live by bread alone but by every word of life coming from God.

'If you are the Son of God, throw yourself down from the pinnacle of the Temple' and people open-mouthed will believe in you. Here is outlined a second basic human hunger or desire: the need, likewise legitimate, to be accepted. From it arises another temptation. For this innate need quickly changes into a need to appear important, to shine. The trap is to consider oneself the absolute centre, the hub of the world, to become incapable of listening to any opinion other than one's own, to want to impose one's ideas on others at all costs – for their own good. It is active idolatry substituting for God in all ages.

Jesus could very well have used his power, his gifts, not for himself but simply for the success of his mission by attracting people through his prestige as all-powerful guru. And who knows but that some days when failure was becoming too heavy a burden, he was touched by a breath of that temptation.

But in common with the God of the Covenant respectful of human freedom, Jesus rejects this patently diabolical temptation to use the Word of God, to reduce religion to the miraculous as a media spectacle, or to appropriate it as we sometimes do to justify our wars, our 'apartheid'.

To behave in this way is an act of flat defiance against God. 'You shall not tempt the Lord your God.' The success of his mission will not be the result of an effective publicity campaign exploiting people's religious needs nor of a Church with temporal power, but will be the fruit of a love self-giving to the end and one which never constrains.

'If you bow down before me I will give you the power and glory of all the kingdoms of the world.' Here appears that other hunger, which is after all quite closely linked to the former: the human instinct to dominate the created universe, the legitimate aspiration to surpass others, which can be a source of progress. The trap is the way the need usually degenerates into a crushing abuse of power. The hunger for power knows on occasion how to hide behind the most noble exterior, even the most spiritual. It is not only kings or dictators who like people to bow low before them.

'You shall worship the Lord your God alone.' Humans, if they are not to suffer alienation, must kneel only to a God revealed as the power of love. Jesus had more than once to resist this deviation. He had to refuse those who dreamed of making him king or getting him on their side in ideological disputes.

These three snares or temptations of the Devil express the on-going fight he probably had to wage all his life. Human temptations, then and now. Inspired and driven by the Spirit, the man Jesus, poor, humble, a servant, in our name rejected those traps which can destroy us as human beings and as children of God.

His Easter triumph frees us from falling foul of this triple suicidal snare

27

God's scandalous silences

If God is Word he is also Silence. Not the silence we have been considering, which surrounds and prepares for the Word, but a Silence very like an apparent absence. This 'scandal' of God's silence was already one of the great sources of questioning for the people of the Covenant in the course of their turbulent history. An incomprehensible silence which often arouses an anguished prayer in the psalmist faced with the triumphant arrogance of the wicked:

> O God do not keep silence;
> do not hold your peace or be still, O God! (Ps 83:1).
> Do not be silent, O God of my praise.
> For wicked and deceitful mouths
> are opened against me (Ps 109:1-2).

Even the prophets are sometimes bitter, in revolt at seeing the poor exploited, the innocent always despised, and God remaining silent. They shout at God: 'O Lord, how long, how long shall I cry for help, and you will not listen? Why are you silent when the wicked swallow those more righteous than they?' (Hab 1:2,13).

As for the drama of Job, it has become the most well-known illustration of the unfortunate innocent appealing against the silence of God:

> I cry to you and you do not answer me;
> I stand before you and you merely look at me (Job 30:20).

We should remember that the people of the Bible at the time of the Exile, after the fall of Jerusalem, saw their whole religious universe crumbling, the Promised Land overrun by invaders, the messianic line deported, the Temple in ruins. A terrible shock for faith, which then poses the tormenting question: Where is God? A new and urgent necessity to purify their conception of God, mine the content of his promises and the meaning of his call.

The psalms said to be by the *anawim*, the poor of the Lord, written after that terrible Exile, express this agonising silence on the part of God:

Why do you not reply, Lord! (Ps 10:13)
O God do not keep silence:
do not hold your peace and be still, O God! (Ps 83:1)
How long, O Lord, will you hide your face? (Ps 13:11)
Rouse yourself! Why do you sleep, O Lord? (Ps 43:23)

How are we to live with this scandalous silence of God? How evade the Paschal dimension of solitude, which Jesus himself undertook? Sometimes, then, our solitude will be that mysterious time of ploughing and sowing during which the Spirit patiently fashions our being for eternity. Silence of the womb. Of the new people for the new land. Silence of Holy Saturday awaiting Easter. Silence of despoliation of our poor possessions, our fleeting projects, in order to receive the imperishable riches of God.

Silence of the old nature which dies and the child of God reborn. Silence of the wheat seed buried in earth before becoming a new ear of corn. Silence of the chrysalis preparing the flight of the butterfly. Silence of metamorphosis, of passing on. For there is never any life without growth and growth without transformation, nor transformation without death. Silence will always be at once a dying and a rebirth.

Silence not only of the combat against the forces of evil but also of purification, of fathoming the mystery of God and humanity. God does sometimes seem not to speak. But that silence is only another way of respecting human liberty, inviting us to deepen our desires, enlarge our horizons. If Love sometimes falls silent, it is still a Word of revelation.

If God ardently desires to love me, come to me, fill me, he nevertheless does not want any misunderstanding about what I am to my very core, what he really is, and what he is offering me. When our silence seems empty, when God seems inconsistent and our words directed to him appear hollow foolishness, perhaps that is the moment when the Creator is inviting us to a new stage in our spiritual life.

A difficult journey, in which we have to learn to keep silent for God alone. The temptation then is to ascribe earlier stages to illusion or auto-suggestion. Now the Spirit is leading us through this 'desert stage' towards the next stage, to a new and truer attitude before God.

Terrible silence, purifying our natural longing to acquire, to accumulate spiritual experiences.

Now, it is no more possible to stock up on grace than it was with the manna in the desert. So we have to rediscover the liberality of God's love, his covenant and his gifts. Unpredictable desert experience. Uneasy night. Necessary dryness which confirms us in the humility and the abandonment of faith. Night of the heart and the mind where we begin to doubt everything: ourself, others and God himself. Terrible silence. Night of faith.

Those dramatic stages in the journey of the people of God always ended, as the writings from after the Exile show, in a greater intensity of faith.

But the impression of conducting a solitary monologue at times becomes for some a dramatic struggle
which ends in giving up the faith. André Gide as one
example tells of the inner battle he had to endure in his
adolescence which made him fall into atheism:

'My eternal Lord! Ah, to know you! One remains
long on one's knees and the body is ill at ease while the
soul is searching for new ways to pray, and sometimes
takes fright at the everlasting monologue. What it is to
hear no reply, to believe still, in faith with no assurances;
waiting, praying and sure already that hope is a deception; and praying again in spite of everything because
perhaps.'

François Mauriac tells in one of his novels of the sad
reply of a priest, drowning in the night of disbelief, to a
young seminarian who remarked that he could not love
an idea or a myth all his life:

'One can love a person who died nearly two thousand
years ago, it is true. I am the proof of that, and so are
many others. How he has deceived me! as he has
deceived us through the centuries. 'I have prayed, begged
so hard, made such supplication. At your age we make
up demands on us and responses, and we think it is
God speaking. We don't know that there is no one there!'

These rebellious cries of yesterday and of today before
God's silence are our own at some time or another. When
harsh misfortune seizes upon us, when failure in our
efforts and a time of testing tear us apart, when sickness,
suffering or a death are upon us, the tormenting question
arises in our heart: Where is God in all this?

This human desire to see God intervene when everything is tottering cannot be blamed. But we should see in
it also the temptation of humankind to fabricate a 'useful' God to match our dreams and our fears and at the
service of our immediate needs. Such were the gods

conceived throughout antiquity. And is there no pagan slumbering in each one of us?

If God's apparent silence hurts us it can also be the occasion for a genuine and salutary question: What God do I believe in? A question not to be too quickly answered by intellectual niceties or a pious response.

Besides, this God dreamed up in the service of our loves, our successes, is not resistant to scandal in the present social and cultural context. And in the face of the death of a utility God there are only two possible attitudes left: atheistic indifference or a humble acceptance of a God who is not measuring up to our desires.

Doubt can become the pathway to a purified faith ceaselessly rediscovering the God of Jesus Christ, humbly incarnate as a child and who died, innocent, crucified.

This God is in no sense, certainly not, a simple projection of the human need to cover up our existential anguish. We could never have invented such a God. He in no way conforms to the idea of spontaneous human needs looking for the compensation of religion.

Jesus Christ has desacralised all the false gods of natural religion. In the face of this God who maintains silence we are truly required to make a Paschal exodus. To live our Easter is also to crucify all our conceptions of God in order to accept an always greater God in a freely-given covenant.

The God revealed by Jesus Christ is not 'useful' for anything in the limited sense. He does not eliminate either the bounds or the trials of the human condition but transfigures our every-day and widens our horizons.

How hard it is to convert to the God of the gospels, to go from the 'pagan' God who must be appeased, cajoled, to the God who takes on our death so that new life may gush forth.

No need to justify God's silences. But these silences of God could be a word hidden, cryptic, which we have to learn to hear and interpret. Again, God's silence is a kind of unspoken word driving us to fathom the tenour of our desires, enlarge the horizon of our needs, admit our radical poverty, accept the free gift of his own life.

This silence-word could be his way of respecting our freedom, of inviting us to grow up and become responsible for our own future jointly with that of others. A father has to draw back, without ever being too far away, for his child to learn to walk.

The believer has no ready-made answers to explain God's silences but since we believe in his love revealed in the words and actions of Jesus Christ, we suspect that these silences must have some meaning which escapes us.

28

Our Lady of silence

Our Lady of Silence,
trusting in your motherly care
I ask you for the grace of silence.

Our Lady of Silence,
you received the power of the Spirit
so as to give flesh to the Word of God.
Grant me the silence of humility
which will allow Love to incarnate
in all the actions of my life
and I attribute nothing of it to myself.

Our Lady of Silence,
at Christmas you contemplated the Child of Bethle-
hem.
Grant me the silence of faith
which welcomes the unpredictable
and sees in every human face the face of God.
Our Lady of Silence,
at the foot of the Cross you mourned the death of your
Son.
Grant me the silence of hope,
hope in God's future,
and the expectation of fruit from the seed which dies.
Our Lady of Silence,
dazzled you entered into Easter light.
Grant me the grace of Paschal joy

to see in the circumstances of daily life
the beginnings of spring and resurrection.

Our Lady of Silence,
with the apostles you prayed to receive the Holy
Spirit.
Grant me the silence of adoration,
opening to the gifts of the living Christ
to bear witness to his Presence anew.

Our Lady of Silence,
you pondered in your heart
on all of life's events,
joyful or sad.
Grant me the silence of watchfulness
to discern in the night the passing of the Lord.

Michel Hubaut

FORGIVENESS

Why is forgiveness necessary? How often should we forgive? How can we forgive without condoning evil? Are there some crimes which are unforgivable! How can we remember without bitterness? Can we forgive someone who shows no sign of remorse? Can society survive without forgiveness?

These are just some of the questions which Michel Hubaut explores using illustrations from his own and others' experiences. While not claiming to provide any easy answers he offers material for reflection, allowing each reader to look into their own conscience.

By a detailed study of the concept of forgiveness in both the Old and New Testaments he explores the particular light shed by the Judeo-Christian revelation. He shows how 'Christian' forgiveness goes beyond human logic, belonging rather to the realm of grace.

Finally, he points out that it is the duty of all Christians to be 'ambassadors' of Christ, sharing with others the forgiveness they have experienced as a free gift of God.

MICHEL HUBAUT, a Franciscan, is a writer and retreat-giver and a contributor to several journals and reviews.

ISBN 085439 475 3   128 pages

John Arnold

THE QUALITY OF MERCY
A fresh look at the Sacrament of Reconciliation

"The sacraments are such vital gifts for the life of the
Church and we must be prepared to question and develop our own understanding of them. This is particularly true in the Sacrament of Reconciliation. Whilst
the years since Vatican II have seen developments in
our theological understanding of this sacrament, I suspect that not enough has been said about how we should
set about using it well or to consider why so many
people apparently no longer choose to use it at all.

This book offers a guide and helps to ask the questions that we should all be addressing about our personal use of the sacrament. It reminds us of the first and
most important element of God's love for us and the
expression of that love through forgiveness and en-
couragement.

Westminster Cathedral has a long tradition in pro-
viding for the celebration of the Sacrament of Reconciliation. It is appropriate that this book comes from a
chaplain at the Cathedral and I welcome the invitation
that it makes to reflect on the importance that this
sacrament can have for each one of us.

I recommend this book to you in the hope that it will
instil a new sense of gratitude for that quality of mercy
which is not strained."

Basil Hume OSB
Cardinal Archbishop of Westminster

085439 433 8   128pp